James

TWENTY STUDIES FOR INDIVIDUALS,
ONE-ON-ONES, AND SMALL GROUPS

BARB RAVELING

Copyright ©2022 Barb Raveling

All rights reserved. No part of this publication may be reproduced, distributed, or transmitted in any form or by any means, including photocopying, recording, or other electronic or mechanical methods, without the prior written permission of the author.

Scripture quotations taken from the (NASB®) New American Standard Bible®, Copyright © 1960, 1971, 1977, 1995 by The Lockman Foundation. Used by permission. All rights reserved. www.lockman.org

Cover Design by Cindy Kiple

Interior Design by Cindy Kiple

ISBN 978-0-9802243-6-8

Introduction 5

1 Benefits of Trials 11
   James 1:1–8

2 The Comparison Game 17
   James 1:9–11

3 Overcoming Temptation 23
   James 1:12–18 14

4 Slow to Anger 29
   James 1:19–21

5 Hearers and Doers 35
   James 1:22–25

6 Real Religion vs. Fake Religion 41
   James 1:26–27

7 Playing Favorites 49
   James 2:1–13

8 Faith and Works 55
   James 2:14–20

9 Making God First 61
   James 2:21–24

10 Taking Risks for God 71
   James 2:24–26

11 Taming the Tongue 77
   James 3:1–12

12 Jealousy and Selfish Ambition 83
   James 3:13–18

13 Envy and Lust 89
   James 4:1–6

14 Spiritual Attack 95
   James 4:7–10

15 Letting Go of Judgment 101
   James 4:11–12

16 Pursuing Goals 107
   James 4:13–17

17 Holding Money with Open Hands 113
   James 5:1–6

18 Trials and Maturity 119
   James 5:7–11

19 Praying, Praising, and Healing 125
   James 5:12–15

20 Prayers and Confession 131
   James 5:16–20

About the Author 137

Introduction

Have you ever read the same Bible passage multiple times because you couldn't get your brain to focus? This Bible study is the result of one of those mornings for me. I was sipping coffee, my Bible on my lap, and for the life of me, I just couldn't concentrate. *Maybe if I write a few questions,* I thought, *it will be easier to focus on the passage.*

I did that—and I loved the process. Not only did the questions help me focus, even before my coffee kicked in, they also helped me mature and grow closer to God as I used the questions to work through my real-life problems. The book you have in front of you is a result of that morning with God, and it's the first book in a series of Bible studies.

ABOUT THE SERIES

I call the series Transformation Bible Studies because these studies are all about transformation—studying God's Word in a way that will change your life. Not just in a general sense, but in your day-to-day struggles, habits, temptations, and trials.

Each day we'll look at a small section of Scripture, and I'll provide questions you can use to apply the passage to something that's going on in your life right now. It may be something you've been struggling with for a long time, something small that happened yesterday, or something that's not even on your radar right now—but James thinks it should be!

I'm hoping you'll use the questions to cozy up into God's lap and talk over your problems with Him. At the end of each study, I'll give you a prayer suggestion, then ask you to identify your biggest takeaway.

The term *takeaway* is one we use in life coaching. Basically, it means, what was your aha moment? Where did the Holy Spirit give you insight or pour out truth? Often, I'll learn a new insight just by answering that question.

I'll also ask if you'd like to take any action steps based on that day's lesson. While it's helpful to ask and answer this question, don't be alarmed if you can't follow through on all of your action steps. James talks about so many different topics in this book that every lesson could be a new project—and it's impossible to change everything at once!

So go ahead and answer the question, work on what you can work on at the moment, but don't stress if you can't do everything. In doing this study with my husband and some of our friends, I found that it's helpful for growth even if we can't change everything at once.

ABOUT THE STUDY

One purpose of Bible study is to know God's Word and what it means. To fulfill that purpose, we study the Greek and Hebrew meanings of words and look at other passages that tie in with the passage we're reading. This helps us to get to know the Word, and I love Bible studies like that.

But another purpose of Bible study is to take in the truth of God's Word and apply it to our lives so we can grow in holiness. That's what this Bible study is about. Instead of having Greek and Hebrew definitions and lots of questions about the passage itself and related Bible verses, I'll be asking questions to help you apply the passage to a current struggle you're facing.

It might be a temptation, a big trial, or something small that happened to you yesterday. Use the Bible passage to understand your situation and brainstorm ways to deal with it based on the Scripture. I'll provide questions to walk you through the process.

I always begin each lesson with this question: Summarize or diagram this passage. Use this question in whatever way works best for you to learn the essence of the Bible passage. I've included the main Scripture passage in each lesson, which will make it easier to answer the questions, but you'll also need a Bible if you'd like to look up some of the other references.

Following is an example of how my husband, Scott, and I summarized James 5:12–14. You can see that they're very different because of our personalities and what we focused on in the passage.

> *But above all, my brothers and sisters, do not swear, either by heaven or by earth or with any other oath; but your yes is to be yes, and your no, no, so that you do not fall under judgment. Is anyone among you suffering?* Then *he must pray. Is anyone cheerful? He is to sing praises. Is anyone among you sick?* Then *he must call for the elders of the church and they are to pray over him, anointing him with oil in the name of the Lord.*

Barb's diagram:
- Don't swear by heaven or earth → yes be yes and no be no.
- Suffering → Pray
- Cheerful → Sing praises
- Sick → Call the elders of the church to pray over you and anoint you with oil
- Prayer of faith → restores the one who is sick → the Lord will raise him up. If he's committed sins, they'll be forgiven him.

Scott's summary:
- Don't make promises you can't keep.
- Don't be wishy-washy.
- Pray, pray, and pray.

Do you see how different our summaries are? I diagram and Scott summarizes. When Scott summarizes a passage, he's looking for the bottom line. When I diagram a passage, I'm looking for relationships—if/then (example: if you're suffering, then pray), command/promise, etc. I also look for guiding principles, definitions, characteristics of

God, different ways to love well, or anything else that strikes my eye.

Do whatever will help you learn the essence of the passage. If you'd like to see more examples of diagramming a passage, check out this link: https://barbraveling.com/how-to-meditate-on-scripture/.

ABOUT JAMES

Before we begin, let's take a quick look at the book we'll be studying. James was written around AD 48 and was probably the first book written in the New Testament. It was most likely written by James, the oldest half-brother of Jesus. This is significant because it's the only book of the Bible written by someone who lived in the same house as Jesus growing up!

Think of your own brothers and sisters. Were any of them well behaved enough that you would have been willing to believe they were God? Yet, James did. He believed so strongly that Jesus was God that he was martyred for his belief in AD 62, according to Josephus, a first-century Jewish historian.

The book of James was written to Jewish believers in the early church. It's a practical book, filled with tips that help new believers mature. James deals with real-life issues, so it's a great book to study if we want to work through our current struggles.

INDIVIDUALS, ONE-ON-ONES, AND SMALL GROUPS

This Bible study is an effective tool for individuals, one-on-ones (two people), and small groups if the members know one another well (or want to know the others better). Because some of the questions are personal, it's most useful for groups in which participants are willing to open up to one another and also for people who welcome growth. It can lead to great discussions as the lessons cover topics we all struggle with.

If you're doing the study by yourself, use it as a time to commune with God and go to Him for help with life. Because James is so cut-and-dried about what to do and not do, you may be tempted to beat yourself up when you see your shortcomings through the eyes of the Bible passage.

If you're tempted to do that, remember that all of us struggle with sin and weakness and that God is a God of grace (Romans 3:23; 7:15–20; Hebrews 4:14–16). Beating ourselves up is fruitless, but going to God for help with transformation is life-changing.

This is also a great study for one-on-ones since it deals with real-life issues. It could be used with a friend, family member, or in a mentoring relationship, such as a mentor/mentee, campus ministry leader/student, or youth group leader/student. If you use this book to mentor someone, I suggest having both of you do the studies each week so you're both working toward growth in the same areas of your life.

LEADING A GROUP STUDY

To lead a group study, ask the participants to do the studies on their own at home, then go through the questions one by one when you meet. If you find after the first couple of classes that you never get to all the questions (this was true for my group), choose the questions you want to cover ahead of time. One question we always included was "What was your biggest takeaway?" as it was interesting to see how God worked differently in each of our lives through that week's study.

If you don't have twenty weeks for your class, you can do the study with the following options: 1) Choose the lessons you want to cover, still doing one per week, and let class members do others on their own; 2) let each group member choose one or two lessons they'd like to discuss and just do those lessons; or 3) assign more than one lesson per week and discuss the highlights of each lesson as you won't have time for a full discussion. You could do that by asking these questions: What stood out to you in this lesson? What challenged you most? What did you find hardest to answer? Why? This may not lead to as deep of a discussion, but it will allow you to cover more lessons.

Since a couple of personal questions are included in each study, be sensitive when asking how individuals answered them. Let class members share details if they'd like or withhold them if they'd rather not share personal things.

Always be loving and gentle, recognizing that people are at different points in their walks with God and they have different personalities. While one class member might be willing to share everything in her life, another class member will have a hard time sharing personal things. That's okay. There are still many opportunities for growth from both the group discussion and doing the lessons at home with God.

My prayer is that this study will lead to many wonderful times with God and opportunities to go to Him for help with your daily struggles—and also wonderful times of deep fellowship with others if you do it with a group or another person.

ONE

Benefits of Trials

JAMES 1:1–8

1 James, a bond-servant of God and of the Lord Jesus Christ, To the twelve tribes who are dispersed abroad: Greetings. 2 Consider it all joy, my brethren, when you encounter various trials, 3 knowing that the testing of your faith produces endurance. 4 And let endurance have its perfect result, so that you may be perfect and complete, lacking in nothing. 5 But if any of you lacks wisdom, let him ask of God, who gives to all generously and without reproach, and it will be given to him. 6 But he must ask in faith without any doubting, for the one who doubts is like the surf of the sea, driven and tossed by the wind. 7 For that man ought not to expect that he will receive anything from the Lord, 8 being a double-minded man, unstable in all his ways.

OBSERVE

1. Summarize or diagram this passage. (See Introduction for the explanation of how to do this. If you'd rather just record notes as you read the passage, that works, too!)

THINK

2. This passage is probably the most famous passage on trials in the Bible. What do you think of when you hear the word *trial?*

3. When I think of trials, I think of things that wear me down and make me miserable. Yet James tells us to count it all joy when we encounter trials. What's James's bottom line about why we can be joyful about trials?

ONE BENEFIT OF TRIALS is that they can help us grow. We often hear the phrase *trials make us grow*, but it's one of those phrases that goes in one ear and out the other. We've heard it so often, we no longer think about what it means. Instead, we think of growth in a generic sense—we'll be a stronger Christian after the trial. Yet when we look at the things James (and Jesus) talked about in the Bible, they're practical areas of growth: things like don't judge, stop worrying, let go of your anger, stop being selfish, and help those in need (Matthew 5:22–24; 6:25–34; Luke 6:27–38; John 15:12–13; James 3:13–18; 4:11–12).

4. Why do you think James and Jesus want believers to grow in practical ways (i.e., be perfect and complete, lacking in nothing)?

5. The interesting thing is that trials can help us grow in character and faith, but they can also help us grow in the fruit of the Spirit if we walk in the Spirit during our trials (Galatians 5:16, 22–23). Let's see what this would look like in real life. Begin by listing some of your current trials, both big and small—anything that is messing up your life or making you unhappy, worried, stressed, annoyed, etc.

6. Now take two or three trials from that list and share how God could use each of those trials to help you grow in character and fruit of the Spirit (love, peace, joy, self-control, etc.). Be specific.

7. When you think of all the ways you could grow from those trials, is it easier to count them all joy—or to even think the trial might be worth it for the growth (depending on the trial)? Explain.

8. Let's take a few painful minutes to see if the way we're currently responding to our trials will help us grow and lead to the benefits we mentioned in question 6. List two or three trials below (from question 6) and record how you are currently responding to those trials in your behavior, thoughts, and actions.

9. Do you think what you're currently doing will lead to perfect and complete, lacking in nothing? If not, what will it lead to?

 **PRAY**

10. Read through today's Bible passage again with your trials in mind, then ask God for wisdom in how to handle them in a way that will help you grow. You can either write your prayer in the space below or just visit with God without writing anything down.

 TAKEAWAY

11. What is your biggest takeaway from today's lesson?

 ACTION STEPS

12. List any action steps you'd like to take based on your takeaway and prayer time with God.

TWO
The Comparison Game
JAMES 1:9–11

9 But the brother of humble circumstances is to glory in his high position; 10 and the rich man is to glory in his humiliation, because like flowering grass he will pass away. 11 For the sun rises with a scorching wind and withers the grass; and its flower falls off and the beauty of its appearance is destroyed; so too the rich man in the midst of his pursuits will fade away.

OBSERVE

1. Summarize or diagram this passage. (See Introduction for the explanation of how to do this. If you'd rather just record notes as you read the passage, that works, too!)

THINK

2. In a day of social media and ratings galore, we're often tempted to compare ourselves with others. We all fall into the "rich person" position in some areas of our lives and the "poor person" (humble) position in others. List some areas of your life where you look around and think, *You know, I'm pretty good in this area!* (For example, are you smart, efficient, attractive, creative, etc.? Do you have a satisfying lifestyle, good health, a great job, etc.?)

3. Now list some areas of your life where you fall into the poor-person position. These could be things you don't do well, areas where you feel like you're at the bottom of the pack, or areas where you receive judgment. (For example, in many circles being a Christian will put you into a poor-person position, especially if you're a conservative Christian.)

4. Can you think of any dangers or temptations of being in the rich-person position when it comes to a) your relationship with God, b) your relationship with others, and c) how you feel about yourself? For example, sometimes when we're at the top, we're tempted to rely on our

own strength rather than God's, or we might base our identity and/or happiness on things that don't last.

5. Can you think of any dangers or temptations of being in the poor-person position when it comes to a) your relationship with God, b) your relationship with others, and c) how you feel about yourself? For example, sometimes when we're at the bottom, we feel we can't be happy until we reach the top. Or we may assume others won't like or respect us since we're at the bottom, and this can keep us from reaching out to them.

6. Even though we're rich and poor in different areas of our lives, we have a tendency to see ourselves as one way or another because we focus on just one or two areas. Are you currently seeing yourself as rich (at the top) or poor (at the bottom)? What areas of your life are you focusing on that make you see yourself in that position?

7. In your eyes, how does the world see you? Is that really how the world sees you or could you just be imagining it?

WHETHER WE FEEL like winners, losers, or somewhere in between, James gives us all the same advice: *Don't define yourself by how you stack up against others.* Why? Because the world's evaluation tools (riches, good looks, job success, etc.) will all fade away. The important thing is who you are in God's eyes.

8. Based on what you've read in Scripture (not on how you feel in your gut), how do you think God sees you? (If you need ideas for how God sees you, check out this link: https://barbraveling.com/insecurity-bible-verses/.)

9. Based on what the Bible says, how does God's view of you compare with the way you think the world sees you from question 7?

10. Think of one of the situations you listed in question 3. How would it change your attitude, actions, and enjoyment of life if you were to see yourself as God sees you (question 8) and care about what God cares about on a regular basis?

HERE'S THE WONDERFUL TRUTH: God (the richest One alive) doesn't see you as rich or poor. Instead, He sees you as you are—rich *and* poor: a glorious, interesting, unique creation with areas of great character while also a sinner who messes up on a regular basis. And the wonderful thing is that even though He sees you as you are in the sin and weakness department, He doesn't focus on that because He sees you through eyes of grace.

 PRAY

11. Read through today's Bible passage again, then spend time glorying in your position in Christ. Thank God for your eternal destination and the chance to see Him face-to-face. You can either write your prayer in the space below or just visit with God without writing anything down.

 **TAKEAWAY**

12. What is your biggest takeaway from today's lesson?

 ACTION STEPS

13. List any action steps you'd like to take based on your takeaway and prayer time with God.

THREE

Overcoming Temptation

JAMES 1:12–18

12 Blessed is a man who perseveres under trial; for once he has been approved, he will receive the crown of life which the Lord has promised to those who love Him. 13 No one is to say when he is tempted, "I am being tempted by God"; for God cannot be tempted by evil, and He Himself does not tempt anyone. 14 But each one is tempted when he is carried away and enticed by his own lust. 15 Then when lust has conceived, it gives birth to sin; and sin, when it has run its course, brings forth death. 16 Do not be deceived, my beloved brothers and sisters. 17 Every good thing given and every perfect gift is from above, coming down from the Father of lights, with whom there is no variation or shifting shadow. 18 In the exercise of His will He gave us birth by the word of truth, so that we would be a kind of first fruits among His creatures.

OBSERVE

1. Summarize or diagram this passage.

THINK

2. Since this passage is about temptation, let's begin by exploring our temptations. Each of us will have different temptations according to our personalities, upbringing, and trials. Think of your current life and the way you respond to trials. List some of your temptations, including heart temptations, such as a temptation to worry, resent people, dwell on the negative, live in regret, or be envious of your friends. Review question 5 from Lesson 1 if you need help remembering your trials.

3. Verses 14 and 15 give us an understanding of how temptation works. It's not God who tempts us; it's our desires. Look over your temptation list and choose two temptations to work on for today's study. For each temptation, list a desire that may be fueling that temptation. For example, a temptation to worry about money may be fueled by a desire for financial security. A temptation to spend too much time on social media may be fueled by a desire for connection. A temptation to binge on Netflix may be fueled by a desire for the fun and easy life.

4. In question 3 we looked at what we hope we'll get (or avoid) if we indulge our desires—things like a great life, a finished to-do list, or being able to stay in our comfort zone. Yet James 1:15 tells us we'll get death if we give in to a temptation that leads to sin. This death is eternal if we give up on God altogether, but we can also experience temporary death as believers—the death of abundant life (John 10:10)—as giving in to temptation leads to things like negative emotions, addictions, immaturity, and distance from God. Look at the first temptation you listed in question 3 and the desire that's fueling your temptation. How does giving in to that temptation affect a) your enjoyment of life and your health, b) your ministry and/or relationships with others, and c) your relationship with God?

5. Look at the second temptation you listed in question 3 and the desire that's fueling your temptation. How does giving in to that temptation affect a) your enjoyment of life and your health, b) your ministry and/or relationships with others, and c) your relationship with God?

6. Verse 8 says that every good gift comes from the Father. We see these gifts in the fruit of the Spirit—love, joy, peace, etc. (Galatians 5:22–23)—and other things He gives us. Review your answers to question 3. What "gifts" are you usually looking for with each of your temptations? What gift does God want to give you? (For example, when I give in to the temptation to procrastinate my work, I'm looking for the "gift" of the easy life. God, on the other hand, wants to give me the gifts of the fruit of the Spirit and personal growth—in this case, the fruit of self-control and personal growth in the area of doing my work.)

7. How do God's gifts (the fruit of the Spirit, a closer walk with Him, abundant life, sharing in His ministry, personal growth, etc.) differ from the sorts of gifts we go looking for?

8. If we struggle with the same temptation for a long time, it's tempting to just give up trying to fight it. Yet James 1:12 tells us that the man is blessed who perseveres under trial. This could also be translated "blessed is the man who perseveres under temptation." Why would

the person who perseveres with overcoming his or her temptations be more blessed than the one who gives up and stops working on overcoming them?

9. Choose one of the temptations you mentioned in this lesson. What would it look like to persevere with overcoming it? For example, if I were to persevere in overcoming the temptation of procrastination, I might try to develop the habit of communing with God while I write, going to Him for help when I don't feel like writing, and seeking His opinion rather than the imagined opinions of everyone else. I might also listen to Ted Talks on how to overcome procrastination, get a book on how to overcome it, or do an internet search for "procrastination Bible" to see how others deal with it. (Of course, I would have to be careful not to search Ted Talks and books on procrastination *instead* of doing my work, as we all know what that rabbit hole looks like!)

PRAY

10. Read the passage one last time with your temptations in mind, then visit with God about your temptations. Ask Him for the strength and truth, as well as practical ideas, to gain victory over your temptations.

TAKEAWAY

11. What is your biggest takeaway from today's lesson?

ACTION STEPS

12. List any action steps you'd like to take based on your takeaway and prayer time with God. If you'd like help with overcoming temptation, check out the Break a Habit or Live in Peace tabs at barbraveling.com.

FOUR
Slow to Anger

JAMES 1:19–21

19 This you know, my beloved brethren. But everyone must be quick to hear, slow to speak and slow to anger; 20 for the anger of man does not achieve the righteousness of God. 21 Therefore, putting aside all filthiness and all that remains of wickedness, in humility receive the word implanted, which is able to save your souls.

 **OBSERVE**
1. Summarize or diagram this passage.

THINK

2. According to this passage, what does anger not do? What does the Word do?

3. Verse 19 talks about being quick to hear and slow to speak. List the people in your life who would benefit if you were to follow this advice.

4. What kinds of things do you say in those relationships that you probably shouldn't say?

5. James 1:20 says that anger doesn't produce the righteousness of God. Let's see if this holds true in our own lives. How do people respond when you're angry with them (or when you say the things you men-

tioned in the previous question)? Does it cause them to recognize their own sin, repent, grow closer to God, and be more like Him? If not, how do they usually respond?

6. What might change about those relationships if you were quick to hear and slow to speak?

7. Our anger doesn't produce righteousness in the lives of others, but it also doesn't produce righteousness in our own lives. Think of the days you feel irritated or annoyed. How does it affect your attitude and actions? What would happen if you were to let go of your anger and forgive the person you're angry with? How might you be different?

8. Often we don't want to let go of anger and forgive people because we think they'll get away with their bad behavior if we do that. We also think that if we let it go, they'll never change. Review your answers to question 5. Have you been good at getting people to change by hanging on to your irritation, anger, or annoyance (or by saying the things you say in question 4)? Explain.

9. Romans 2:4 tells us that the kindness of God leads us to repentance. What would happen if you followed the practice of Romans 2:4 in the relationships you mentioned in question 3, rather than the things you currently say? Invite God to show you what fruit your kindness might bear.

10. Think about the relationships you mentioned in question 3. What would you like to change about the way you respond and relate to those people? (For example, would you like to give more grace, focus on their good traits, wait five seconds before you respond when you're annoyed, etc.?) Explain.

11. In verse 21, James tells us to put away all filth and rampant wickedness. It's unclear whether he's switching to a new topic or describing anger as filth and rampant wickedness, but it is clear what the solution is: In humility, receive the word implanted which is able to save your souls. Think of the relationships you've been working through in this lesson. In what ways do you need to practice humility in those relationships? Offer specific examples of how you can practice humility in each one.

PRAY

12. Keeping in mind the people who annoy you, read through today's Bible passage again. Visit with God about what you learned in today's lesson and anything you'd like to change about the way you handle the relationships you mentioned in today's lesson.

 **TAKEAWAY**

13. What is your biggest takeaway from today's lesson?

 **ACTION STEPS**

14. List any action steps you'd like to take based on your takeaway and prayer time with God.

FIVE

Hearers and Doers

JAMES 1:22–25

22 But prove yourselves doers of the word, and not merely hearers who delude themselves. 23 For if anyone is a hearer of the word and not a doer, he is like a man who looks at his natural face in a mirror; 24 for once he has looked at himself and gone away, he has immediately forgotten what kind of person he was. 25 But one who looks intently at the perfect law, the law of liberty, and abides by it, not having become a forgetful hearer but an effectual doer, this man will be blessed in what he does.

 OBSERVE

1. Summarize or diagram this passage.

THINK

2. List the characteristics of people who read the Bible but don't follow any of the commands (hearers only) and the characteristics of those who read the Bible and work on making necessary changes in their lives (doers).

3. Verse 22 says that hearers are deceiving themselves. Can you think of any lies they might believe that would cause them not to do what the Bible tells them to do? (For example, they may be thinking, *I'm good enough as is,* or, *Everyone else is doing this, so it must be okay.*)

4. According to the passage, what are the benefits of doing what the Bible says rather than just reading it? Can you give an example of this in your own life?

5. Some people say that rules make them want to rebel. For them, rules are the opposite of freedom. Yet this passage speaks of the Bible's "rules" as the law of freedom. It implies that if we do what the Bible tells us to do, we'll be free. Let's see if this holds true in our lives. Think of a time in the last few days when you a) wanted to do something God didn't want you to do or b) didn't want to do something He *did* want you to do. (If you can't think of anything, think of a situation that made you feel irritated, stressed, envious, worried, hopeless, or insecure.) Describe the situation.

6. How do you *feel* like responding in that situation? (Or how did you already respond?)

7. How do you think God wants you to respond to this situation? Why do you think He wants you to respond that way?

Hearers and Doers

8. Now let's take a minute to look at the perfect law, the law of freedom. What does the Bible say about how you should respond in that situation? List any scriptures that come to mind. (Note: If the Bible doesn't say anything specific about what you're struggling with, think of general biblical principles that may speak into your situation, such as "Seek first the kingdom of God.")

9. Would you feel more free or less free if you responded the way the Bible tells you to respond? Why?

10. Review James 1:2–4. How would responding God's way help you grow in maturity?

11. Verse 25 says that if we become active doers of the law of freedom, we'll be blessed in what we do. Can you think of any other blessings that may come from doing what the Word tells you to do in this situation?

PRAY
12. Read through today's Bible passage again with the situation you mentioned in today's lesson in mind. Spend time visiting with God about this situation, using the Bible verses you mentioned in question 8 as a springboard for that conversation.

TAKEAWAY
13. What is your biggest takeaway from today's lesson?

 **ACTION STEPS**

14. List any action steps you'd like to take based on your takeaway and prayer time with God.

SIX
Real Religion vs. Fake Religion

JAMES 1:26–27

26 If anyone thinks himself to be religious, yet does not bridle his tongue but deceives his own heart, this person's religion is worthless. 27 Pure and undefiled religion in the sight of our God and Father is this: to visit orphans and widows in their distress, and to keep oneself unstained by the world.

OBSERVE

1. Summarize or diagram this passage.

THINK

2. James begins this passage by telling his readers that they need to bridle their tongues—or in today's language, they need to stop saying everything that pops into their heads. Do you struggle more with saying things you shouldn't say or with *not* saying things you should say (some examples of this would be not engaging in conversation, not speaking up in situations where you should speak up, or not being proactive in reaching out to people with your words)? Explain

JAMES SAYS WE DECEIVE OURSELVES when we say anything that comes to mind. We could do this in several ways. First, we might think we're great Christians (or religious, as James puts it) because we go to church every time the doors are open, read our Bibles every day, and live a moral life, not realizing that the words we say often hurt people. Second, we might think certain things need to be said when God doesn't agree with us. And finally, we may give unsolicited advice, thinking we're being helpful when we're really annoying people or making them feel insecure.

3. Can you think of some examples from your own life of hurting people with your words or hurting people by not saying enough words? Who could you love better if you were to bridle your tongue or speak more words?

4. This passage contrasts what religion is versus what it's not. What is it, and what isn't it?

ONE WAY JAMES DEFINES RELIGION is to visit orphans and widows in their distress. There are numerous ways we could do this. For example, we could invite a widow or widower for dinner, volunteer at Meals on Wheels, become a foster parent, or sponsor a child through Compassion International. We could also contribute financially to an orphanage or go on a mission trip to serve in an orphanage. Our opportunities to serve depend on our stage of life, community, and resources. Let's see what this looks like in your life.

5. Can you think of any ways you're currently helping orphans, widows, or needy people in your community, work, or the world? Can you think of any other ways you might like to help?

6. Visiting orphans and widows is a practical way to love people, but we can also think of practical ways to love all the people in our lives. Think of the people you know (family, friends, neighbors, and the people who live in your home). What are some practical ways to love those people?

7. It's easy to see how visiting orphans and widows is pure and undefiled religion, but James also mentions keeping oneself unstained by the world. What do you think James means by this?

8. Why is it important to keep ourselves unstained by the world?

9. Can you think of any attitudes you've adopted that fall into the "stained by the world" category? For example, I used to think that life was all about having fun, which is a common worldly philosophy. Because of that, I wasn't inclined to serve others since it wasn't fun. This would also hold true for the person who is stained by a worldly philosophy that life is about getting things done. That person may be so busy working that they wouldn't make time to engage in relationships or serve the people in their homes or communities. List some attitudes or philosophies you hold that keep you from serving and loving others well.

10. We can also be stained by the world by the things we do. For example, spending too much time watching television can limit how much time we have to love and serve others. It can also subtly change the way we think as we adopt the philosophies in the shows we watch. Can you think of any behaviors you engage in that either subtly encourage you to adopt worldly philosophies or keep you from having the time or inclination to serve others and love them well? Explain.

11. In our lesson today, we discussed three areas of our lives to work on if we want to grow in our love for others: being careful about what we say, helping people in need, and keeping ourselves unstained by the world. Which area could you use the most help with in this season of your life? Why?

 PRAY

12. In a lesson like this, it can be easy to dwell on our shortcomings. We all have them. Read the passage again with your shortcomings in mind, then visit with God about anything that came up, confessing any sins you recognized, and soaking in His love and grace. Ask Him what He'd like you to work on from today's lesson.

 **TAKEAWAY**

13. What is your biggest takeaway from today's lesson?

 **ACTION STEPS**

14. List any action steps you'd like to take based on your takeaway and prayer time with God.

SEVEN

Playing Favorites

JAMES 2:1–13

1 My brethren, do not hold your faith in our glorious Lord Jesus Christ with an attitude of personal favoritism. 2 For if a man comes into your assembly with a gold ring and dressed in fine clothes, and there also comes in a poor man in dirty clothes, 3 and you pay special attention to the one who is wearing the fine clothes, and say, "You sit here in a good place," and you say to the poor man, "You stand over there, or sit down by my footstool," 4 have you not made distinctions among yourselves, and become judges with evil motives? 5 Listen, my beloved brethren: did not God choose the poor of this world to be rich in faith and heirs of the kingdom which He promised to those who love Him? 6 But you have dishonored the poor man. Is it not the rich who oppress you and personally drag you into court? 7 Do they not blaspheme the fair name by which you have been called? 8 If, however, you are fulfilling the royal law according to the Scripture, "You shall love your neighbor as yourself," you are doing well. 9 But if you show partiality, you are committing sin and are convicted by the law as transgressors. 10 For whoever keeps the whole law and yet stumbles in one point, he has become guilty of all. 11 For He who said, "Do not commit adultery," also said, "Do not commit murder." Now if you do not commit adultery, but do commit murder, you have become a transgressor of the law. 12 So speak and so act as those who are to be judged by the law of liberty. 13 For judgment will be merciless to one who has shown no mercy; mercy triumphs over judgment.

 **OBSERVE**

1. Summarize or diagram this passage.

 **THINK**

2. This passage talks about favoritism and judgment. How would you define each word, and what is the difference is between showing favoritism and judging people?

JAMES 2:4 SAYS we become judges when we show favoritism. It's like we're saying, "You're a good guy because you're this," and, "You're a bad guy because you're that." The people in James's life were judging one another based on money. Today, we judge on all kinds of things: appearance, political parties, social media behavior, the type of church people go to, their spending habits, etc. Let's look at our own tendencies in this area.

3. What types of people do you judge? (If you have a hard time answering this question, think of the times you mentally roll your eyes or the people who annoy you—either in real life, on social media, or in the news.)

4. Now let's look at the groups of people we judge one at a time. For each of the groups you mentioned in question 2, answer this question: Are the people in those groups sinning by being in that group, or do they just have a different way of doing things? Explain. (For example, if you judge people who live in a rural area, a city, or a state you don't like, is it a sin to live in those places?)

5. Review your groups from questions 3 and 4. If they *are* sinning by being in that group, are their sins worse than your own sins? Explain.

6. How does your judgment of those people affect your ability to love them well?

7. How does your judgment of them affect your relationship with God?

8. When I find myself judging and condemning people (whether they're sinning or not), God always seems to convict me of my *own* sin of being judgmental. Review verses 9–13. How would the truths in that passage help you to stop judging and condemning the people you mentioned in question 3?

9. In verse 8, James reminds us to love our neighbors as ourselves. Read 1 Corinthians 13:4–7 and choose one group you listed in question 3. What would it look like to live out 1 Corinthians 13:4–7 with that person or group?

> *Love is patient, love is kind and is not jealous; love does not brag and is not arrogant, does not act unbecomingly; it does not seek its own, is not provoked, does not take into account a wrong suffered, does not rejoice in unrighteousness, but rejoices with the truth; bears all things, believes all things, hopes all things, endures all things. (1 Corinthians 13:4–7)*

10. How would it change your relationship and attitude toward that person or group if you were to love them with a 1 Corinthians love?

11. What is one thing you could do to overcome your spirit of judgment toward the person or group you judge?

 **PRAY**

12. Read the passage again with the people you tend to judge in mind, then visit with God about anything that came up in today's lesson, or try praying through 1 Corinthians 13:4–7 with the person or group in mind that you mentioned in question 3.

 **TAKEAWAY**

13. What is your biggest takeaway from today's lesson?

 **ACTION STEPS**

14. List any action steps you'd like to take based on your takeaway and prayer time with God.

EIGHT

Faith and Works

JAMES 2:14–20

14 What use is it, my brethren, if someone says he has faith but he has no works? Can that faith save him? 15 If a brother or sister is without clothing and in need of daily food, 16 and one of you says to them, "Go in peace, be warmed and be filled," and yet you do not give them what is necessary for their body, what use is that? 17 Even so faith, if it has no works, is dead, being by itself. 18 But someone may well say, "You have faith and I have works; show me your faith without the works, and I will show you my faith by my works." 19 You believe that God is one. You do well; the demons also believe, and shudder. 20 But are you willing to recognize, you foolish fellow, that faith without works is useless?

OBSERVE

1. Summarize or diagram this passage.

ONE THING I LOVE ABOUT THE BIBLE is that it speaks to all types of people. In this passage, James speaks to those who feel they have no responsibility to change, grow, or serve when they become Christians. He tells them, "You need to do some works, guys! Faith should change the way you live life!" In other passages, Paul speaks to those who do feel a responsibility to serve and grow (Romans 7:15-20; Ephesians 2:1–9). Their problem is that they fall into the trap of thinking they have to be perfect for God to love them. To that group of people, Paul says, "You're saved by grace, you guys, not works! You don't need to be perfect for God to love you!"

 THINK

2. Which attitude—you have no responsibility to serve and grow, or you have to be perfect for God to love you—do you lean toward at the gut level? How does that attitude affect your relationship with God?

3. How does that attitude (you have no responsibility to serve and grow or you have to be perfect for God to love you) affect your relationships with others and your desire to serve others in practical ways? (The interesting thing is that both attitudes can affect service—one because we don't feel the responsibility to serve and the other because we either resent having to serve or feel like we're not perfect enough to serve.)

4. What Scripture passages or truths do you need to remember to help you examine your life in a way that would encourage you to work on your areas of weakness rather than a) beat yourself up because you're not doing enough or perfect enough, or b) not think it's a big deal if you don't serve or grow because God loves you anyway? (Think of your own verses first but if you need help, check out these: Psalm 139:13–18; Jeremiah 31:3–26; Ephesians 2:8–9; Philippians 2:3–8; 3:7–11; Hebrews 4:15–16; 1 Peter 1:16; 1 John 1:9; 3:16–18).

5. James lists three very different examples of works in James 2:14-26. In some ways, the example he mentions in this passage (vv. 14–20) is the easiest to do: feed and clothe the poor. In what ways do you currently feed and clothe the poor? Can you think of anything else God may want you to do?

6. Do you serve people in other ways? List the specific ways you go out of your way to help others. (Don't forget to include the ways you serve in your daily job or occupation.)

SOME OF US ARE ALL ABOUT SERVICE. We always say yes when someone asks us to do things, and we tend to overbook because we're so busy serving. What we really need is rest and rejuvenation because we're good at serving. Others of us are all about being comfy and enjoying life. We tend to do what we feel like doing while not feeling obligated to serve others. What we really need is to serve because we're already good at rest and rejuvenation.

7. Let's see what this looks like in our own lives. What is your tendency, and what do you need more of?

8. How would it help you to love others better if you were to do more of what you recorded in the previous question?

9. If your tendency is to serve all the time, what are some things you could do on a weekly or daily basis to rest and rejuvenate? If your tendency is to rest and rejuvenate, what are some things you could do on a weekly or daily basis to serve?

10. Whether you tend to serve too much or rest too much, it's easy to fall into the trap of doing big service projects—serving the community, church, people at work, or world at large—while ignoring those in your home or other close relationships. Can you think of some ways God may want you to serve the people you're closest to?

 **PRAY**

11. Read the passage again with your own tendencies in mind, then visit with God about how He might like you to get involved in feeding and clothing the poor, serving in other ways, or taking time to rest and rejuvenate.

 TAKEAWAY

12. What is your biggest takeaway from today's lesson?

 ACTION STEPS

13. List any action steps you'd like to take based on your takeaway and prayer time with God.

NINE

Making God First

JAMES 2:21–24

21 Was not Abraham our father justified by works when he offered up Isaac his son on the altar? 22 You see that faith was working with his works, and as a result of the works, faith was perfected; 23 and the Scripture was fulfilled which says, "And Abraham believed God, and it was reckoned to him as righteousness," and he was called the friend of God. 24 You see that a man is justified by works and not by faith alone.

OBSERVE

1. Summarize or diagram this passage.

USUALLY, WHEN I THINK OF WORKS, I think of doing things for God. Yet in today's scripture, James gives another example of works: making God first in our lives. James illustrates this with the story of Abraham and Isaac. Since we know that God was vehemently opposed to child sacrifice,[1] we might ask the question, "Why did God ask Abraham to do this?"[2] I think He did it to give us a visual image of what it looks like to be willing to give everything up for Him—even the things we love most. Let's see what this looks like in our own lives.

 THINK

2. Most of us have things we feel we need to have to be happy. I call these our have-to-haves. It may be good friends, fun and excitement, success (in whatever way you define it), control, financial security, not having to leave your comfort zone, or any number of things. List the things you feel you must have to be happy.[3] Then circle up to three of them to explore for the remainder of this lesson.

3. Now look back at the things you circled in the previous question. How do you respond when you don't get those things (or fear you won't get them in the future)? (For example, do you complain, blame, obsess, stress, withdraw, control, go into perfectionism mode, procrastinate decisions, or turn to things like food, alcohol, or entertain-

ment to escape? These are just a few of our common coping techniques when we don't get what we want.)

USUALLY, WE ENGAGE in these coping techniques because we think we won't be happy unless we get what we want. Abraham was no different. One of Abraham's have-to-haves was a son. God had already told Abraham that He would give him a son, but Sarah was in her late seventies with no kids in sight. So Sarah took matters into her own hands and said, "Abe, take my maid Hagar and have sex with her so we can get ourselves a son."[4] It's interesting to note that Abraham's trial at that point wasn't necessarily not having a son; it was Sarah pressing him to have sex with Hagar. Rather than trusting God and waiting on God's timing, Abraham went into people-pleasing mode and did what Sarah suggested.

4. My guess is that Abraham thought he'd be happier if he did what Sarah (and possibly he also) wanted. Do you think Abraham ended up happier by pursuing his have-to-haves of pleasing Sarah and getting a son? Explain. (If you don't know the rest of the story, you can find it in Genesis 16:1–6; 21:9–14.)

5. Now look back at your have-to-haves in question 2. Do you think you'll reach a point in your pursuit of those things where you'll have enough of them to be happy? Why or why not?

6. How would it change your life if you were to consistently rely on God rather than your have-to-haves for happiness, comfort, identity, and security?

7. Even if we do get enough of our have-to-haves to be happy, our pursuit of them can get in the way of loving others well. How did Abraham's actions affect his ability to love Sarah, Hagar, and Ishmael? (Read Genesis 16:3–6 and 21:9–20 to refresh your memory, if necessary.)[5]

Sarah:

Hagar:

Ishmael:

8. Now think of your own pursuit of the have-to-haves you mentioned in question 2. Are those pursuits getting in the way of loving anyone well? Explain.

IF YOU LOOK AT YOUR LIST of have-to-haves in question 2, most of them are probably good things (just like having a son would have been a good thing for Abraham and Sarah). There is nothing wrong with pursuing good things in a non-sinful way. The problem comes when we want those good things too much, and we stomp our little feet and say, "I can't be happy without this!" This leads to all kinds of problems, including doing things God doesn't want us to do. Thankfully, God can use our lack of have-to-haves to help us grow.

9. One way we can grow is to become more proactive in getting our needs met. Sarah was all about getting her needs met, but many of us have the opposite problem. We complain that life is terrible, but we don't do anything to change it. Look back at question 2. Can you see any areas there that could be helped by you being more proactive about meeting those needs? List those areas and two or three things you could do in each area to meet those needs.

10. Another way we can grow when we're not getting what we want is to work on making God first in our lives and maturing in our character, letting go of things like people-pleasing, selfishness, and pride. Let's see if that happened to Abraham. Think of the sex-with-Hagar Abraham versus the Abraham in today's Bible passage. How did Abraham grow from the old days to the time of this passage?

11. Now look back to the areas of your life you circled in question 2. Can you think of any ways God may want you to grow through the trial of not getting what you want?

IN MY OWN LIFE, I usually think I'll be miserable for the rest of my life if I don't get what I want. It's not until after I make the sacrifice that the joy comes in. But this is important: we only experience the joy when we're clinging to God and relying on Him for perspective, comfort, and fellowship in the midst of suffering.

Remember David in the psalms? Over and over we see him starting the psalm distraught, then becoming more joyful by the end of the psalm as he shifts his trust from having life turn out the way he wants to knowing that God will take care of him regardless of the outcome.

An essential part of reaching that joy is to accept the fact that we may not get what we want. Just think of Abraham. He believed God would provide a sacrifice and that he wouldn't have to go through with sacrificing Isaac (Genesis 22:7–8), yet he still had to accept the possibility that he might have to go through with it.

Shadrach, Meshach, and Abednego also believed God would protect them from the fire, yet they still accepted the possibility that He might not (Daniel 3:17-19). Unless we accept the possibility that we may not get what we want, we'll have a hard time finding peace because our minds will keep saying, *No, that will be the end of the world if I don't get what I want.*

12. Think of the things you circled in question 2. What would you have to accept to find peace in the midst of possibly not getting what you want? Be specific.[6]

13. Spend time mentally giving those things up to God, then record how you feel after you do that.

SOMETIMES ACCEPTING what we need to accept feels good right away. We experience an emotional release when we give up things. But other times it's like Jesus in the garden of Gethsemane, and the acceptance process comes with lots of emotional trauma—so don't be alarmed if acceptance didn't come easily when you tried it just now. If it was hard for Jesus, who lived a sinless life, it will be hard for us. For me, it usually involves laying down my have-to-have and remembering that God is enough, even if I don't get what I want.

PRAY

14. Read the passage again with your have-to-haves in mind, then spend some time visiting with God about them and letting go. Confess any sin, and soak in His love, grace, and "enoughness."

TAKEAWAY

15. What is your biggest takeaway from today's lesson?

ACTION STEPS

16. List any action steps you'd like to take based on your takeaway and prayer time with God.

Chapter 9 Footnotes

1. Leviticus 18:21, 20:1–5; Deuteronomy 12:31; 18:10; Jeremiah 7:30–31; Ezekiel 16:20–21.

2. While this example sounds a bit bizarre to our modern ears, sacrificing children to the gods was a common thing in those days. The people back then wouldn't have been thinking, *Oh I can't believe God asked Abraham to do that*. Instead, they would have thought, *I can't believe Abraham didn't follow through on the sacrifice*. It may have even made them wonder, *Maybe we should stop sacrificing our kids*. It's also helpful to remember that God never planned to have Abraham go through with the sacrifice (Genesis 22:14) and that Isaac was most likely a willing participant in the sacrifice. Although the Bible doesn't specify how old Isaac was at the time of the sacrifice, most theologians put him in his twenties or thirties (https://apologeticspress.org/how-old-was-isaac-when-abraham-was-told-to-offer-him). For further study on this passage (including another theory of why God asked Abraham to sacrifice Isaac), check out David Guzik's commentary on Genesis 22 on blueletterbible.org.

3. If you have a hard time answering this question, check out the idolatry quiz at my blog: https://barbraveling.com/do-you-have-an-idol-quiz/.

4. Genesis 15:1-6; 16:1–2.

5. It's also helpful to remember that God still took care of Hagar and Ishmael even though Abraham put them in a terrible position by giving into Sarah's demands back when she wanted Abraham to have sex with Hagar (Genesis 21:14-21). This story also reminds me of how we're all weak and sinful. And if God can give grace to Abraham and Sarah, He can forgive us and give grace to us for our wrongdoings.

6. If you need some ideas of things you may need to accept, check out my book The Renewing of the Mind Project, or download my I Deserve a Donut app and review the emotions section. Each emotion provides questions you can use to see your situation from a biblical perspective as well as ideas of what you may need to accept to find peace.

TEN

Taking Risks for God

JAMES 2:24–26

24 You see that a man is justified by works and not by faith alone. 25 In the same way, was not Rahab the harlot also justified by works when she received the messengers and sent them out by another way? 26 For just as the body without the spirit is dead, so also faith without works is dead.

OBSERVE

1. Summarize or diagram this passage.

🍃 THINK

2. In today's lesson we look at the final example James gives of works: Rahab hiding the spies. Review the account of Rahab in Joshua 2:1–15. Why do you think Rahab hid the spies and let them escape rather than turning them in?

3. What did Rahab risk by hiding the spies?

4. Chances are, you're not living in a culture where you risk death for following God. But you may risk other things. Can you think of some times when the walking out of your faith caused you to risk embarrassment, judgment, being excluded from a group, failure, ridicule, financial loss, or another sacrifice? List some examples throughout your life, if possible.

5. Now think of some times when God *wanted* you to take a risk and you didn't. This could be in the past, or it could be right now. If possible, list some current situations where you feel that God wants you to do something but you're reluctant to do it because of what you might lose. For example, maybe God wants you to pursue a ministry, work on a relationship, get a job, begin a discipling relationship, write a book, or pursue growth in some area of your character or with a recurring sin. You're afraid to do it because you risk failure or hate to give up something that's important to you. Visit with God for a minute about this, then list some of those areas below.

6. What struck me when I read today's scripture is that Rahab feared God more than she feared what her government would do to her if they found out she hid the spies. Her faith fueled her willingness to take risks. Look back at the situations you mentioned in question 5. What fears are keeping you from following through on taking those risks?

7. If you were to focus on one area in question 5 to work on, which one do you think God would choose? Why do you think He would choose that one? If you don't think God has a preference, which one would you choose and why?

8. Review question 6 to see what you would risk by moving ahead in the situation you mentioned in the previous question. Rahab was willing to take the risk to hide the spies because she trusted in God more than in her local government. What would it look like to trust in God for each of the fears you mentioned in your own risky situation?

9. Rahab's willingness to take a risk helped the spies, but it also led to the future safety of both her and her family (Joshua 6:25). What are some possible outcomes God may be seeking by wanting you to take risks in your situation?

PRAY

10. Read the passage again with your possible risk in mind, then ask God for wisdom to know what to do and the strength to do it.

TAKEAWAY

11. What is your biggest takeaway from today's lesson?

ACTION STEPS

12. List any action steps you'd like to take based on your takeaway and prayer time with God.

ELEVEN

Taming the Tongue

JAMES 3:1–12

1 Let not many of you become teachers, my brethren, knowing that as such we will incur a stricter judgment. 2 For we all stumble in many ways. If anyone does not stumble in what he says, he is a perfect man, able to bridle the whole body as well. 3 Now if we put the bits into the horses' mouths so that they will obey us, we direct their entire body as well. 4 Look at the ships also, though they are so great and are driven by strong winds, are still directed by a very small rudder wherever the inclination of the pilot desires. 5 So also the tongue is a small part of the body, and yet it boasts of great things. See how great a forest is set aflame by such a small fire! 6 And the tongue is a fire, the very world of iniquity; the tongue is set among our members as that which defiles the entire body, and sets on fire the course of our life, and is set on fire by hell. 7 For every species of beasts and birds, of reptiles and creatures of the sea, is tamed and has been tamed by the human race. 8 But no one can tame the tongue; it is a restless evil and full of deadly poison. 9 With it we bless our Lord and Father, and with it we curse men, who have been made in the likeness of God; 10 from the same mouth come both blessing and cursing. My brethren, these things ought not to be this way. 11 Does a fountain send out from the same opening both fresh and bitter water? 12 Can a fig tree, my brethren, produce olives, or a vine produce figs? Nor can salt water produce fresh.

OBSERVE
1. Summarize or diagram this passage.

THINK
2. In verses 9 and 10, James talks about cursing people who were created in the image of God. Since James brought it up, we can assume it was a problem for the people he wrote to. Why do you think James is so opposed to using our tongues to curse people?

3. What happens when you continuously say bad things about another person, either in your mind or out loud?

4. Who do you need to stop saying bad things about, either in your mind or out loud? List them below or on a separate piece of paper if you're concerned someone may open this book and read those names.

5. It's been said that when you take something away, it leaves a void, and you need to find something to fill that void. When we stop thinking and saying bad things about people, we need to start thinking and saying good things about them. List three to five good things about two or three of the people you mentioned in question 4.

6. What happened when you wrote down those good things? Did your feelings change toward the person? Explain.

WHEN I DWELL ON THE GOOD IN PEOPLE, I enjoy them far more. I'm also less inclined to say things I shouldn't say because I'm not even thinking those words! There's no doubt we hurt people when we say bad things about them in our minds or out loud, but we also hurt them in other ways by the things we say. It could be unbiblical teaching (James 3:1), unwanted advice, gossip, complaining, being negative, talking too much, unhelpful political discussions, teasing, a disrespectful tone of voice, or any number of things.

7. What kinds of things do you struggle with when it comes to your tongue, and who are the people in your life who bear the brunt of that?

8. How do those behaviors affect the people you mentioned in the previous question, and how do they affect your relationship with them?

9. What kinds of things would you say to the people you mentioned in questions 7 and 8 if you were to instead follow Paul's advice in Ephesians 4:29–32, and how would your words benefit them?

10. How would your relationships and ability to influence those people change if you were to follow the advice in Ephesians?

 **PRAY**

11. Read the passage again with the people you mentioned in questions 4 and 7 in mind, then visit with God about those relationships. Ask Him to give you insight, wisdom, and ideas of how to change the way you interact with your loved ones.

 **TAKEAWAY**

12. What is your biggest takeaway from today's lesson?

 **ACTION STEPS**

13. List any action steps you'd like to take based on your takeaway and prayer time with God.

TWELVE
Jealousy and Selfish Ambition

JAMES 3:13–18

13 Who among you is wise and understanding? Let him show by his good behavior his deeds in the gentleness of wisdom. 14 But if you have bitter jealousy and selfish ambition in your heart, do not be arrogant and so lie against the truth. 15 This wisdom is not that which comes down from above, but is earthly, natural, demonic. 16 For where jealousy and selfish ambition exist, there is disorder and every evil thing. 17 But the wisdom from above is first pure, then peace loving, gentle, reasonable, full of mercy and good fruits, impartial, free of hypocrisy. 18 And the fruit of righteousness is sown in peace by those who make peace.

OBSERVE
1. Summarize or diagram this passage.

THIS PASSAGE SEEMS TO BE talking about God's wisdom vs. man's wisdom. Man's wisdom says things like "life should be fair" and "you deserve the best!" God's wisdom says things like "lay down your lives for others" and "look out for the interests of others" (1 John 3:16; Philippians 2:3–7).

THINK

2. How would man's wisdom be more likely to lead to bitter jealousy and selfish ambition than God's wisdom?

3. I think it's interesting that this passage mentions both jealousy and bitter jealousy. How would you define *jealousy?* How is that different from *bitter jealousy?*

4. Often we're jealous in some areas but not in others. For example, we might be jealous when we see people with great marriages, but it doesn't bother us if they have more money. Or we might be jealous of people who are skinny but not of people who are smart. Can you think of anyone in your life who makes you feel jealous? What is it about that person that causes you to be jealous?

5. Now let's look at ambition. How would you define or describe *selfish ambition?*

OFTEN WE THINK of a ruthless businessman when we think of selfish ambition, but selfish ambition can show up in any area of our lives when we pursue goals without regard to how they affect others. For example, if we're selfishly ambitious in the area of having fun, we'll ignore the boring work around the house and leave it for someone else. If we're selfishly ambitious in the area of getting things done, we may ignore all the people in our lives to finish our to-do lists.

6. Can you think of any areas of your life where you have a tendency to be selfishly ambitious? List those areas and the people you hurt by pursuing your goals and desires at the expense of others. (Try not to slip into self-condemnation, because we all have these areas, and God can help us grow.)

7. Now read today's scripture again and list all the consequences of jealousy and selfish ambition.

8. Review your answers to questions 4 and 6 and choose one area—either jealousy or selfish ambition—to examine, preferably one you're currently experiencing. How has your jealousy or selfish ambition led to bitterness, arrogance, disorder, or every evil thing?

9. Look at the list in verses 17 and 18. What do you need from that list to help you with the struggle you mentioned in the previous question? (See also Philippians 2:1–4, 4:11–13; Matthew 6:33.)

10. What would it look like if you lived out those Bible verses in that situation?

11. How would it change both you and the person you're jealous of, or the people who would benefit, if you were to let go of selfish ambition with your goals?

🍃 PRAY

12. Read through today's Bible passage again with your jealousy or selfish ambition in mind, then spend time visiting with God about anything that came up in today's lesson, confessing any selfish ambition and bitter jealousy, and asking Him to help you change.

🍃 TAKEAWAY

13. What is your biggest takeaway from today's lesson?

🍃 ACTION STEPS

14. List any action steps you'd like to take based on your takeaway and prayer time with God.

THIRTEEN

Envy and Lust

JAMES 4:1–6

1 What is the source of quarrels and conflicts among you? Is not the source your pleasures that wage war in your members? 2 You lust and do not have; so you commit murder. You are envious and cannot obtain; so you fight and quarrel. You do not have because you do not ask. 3 You ask and do not receive, because you ask with wrong motives, so that you may spend it on your pleasures. 4 You adulteresses, do you not know that friendship with the world is hostility toward God? Therefore whoever wishes to be a friend of the world makes himself an enemy of God. 5 Or do you think that the Scripture speaks to no purpose: "He jealously desires the Spirit which He has made to dwell in us"? 6 But He gives a greater grace. Therefore it says, "God is opposed to the proud, but gives grace to the humble."

 **OBSERVE**

1. Summarize or diagram this passage.

THINK

2. James talks about both lust and envy in this passage. How would you define lust? How would you define envy?

3. Often we can tell what we're lusting for by looking at the people we envy. Can you think of anyone you envy right now? It may be a person who has a job you want, a relationship you'd love to be in, a lifestyle you desire, or any number of things. If no one comes to mind, list some people who make you think, *Boy it would be nice to have their lives.* When you think of those people, what do you want that you don't currently have? List those things next to each person's name.

4. James tells us that envy can lead to quarrels and conflicts. Has your envy affected your relationships in any way with the people you envy? Explain.

5. How does your envy of the people you mentioned in question 3 affect your attitude about the blessings God has given you (which, admittedly, are different from those He gave your envied people)?

6. When we envy others, we usually compare the weak areas in our lives with the strong areas in the lives of the people we envy. Yet they also have things in their lives that are less than ideal. Think of the people you mentioned in question 3. What blessings do you have that your envied people don't have?

7. James tells us that we don't have because either we're not asking or we're asking with the wrong motives. Review question 3 to see the types of things you want but don't have. If you were to ask God for things that correspond to two or three of those areas of desire, what would you ask for? (For example, you may ask for money to travel, a great job, or a community of close friends.)

JAMES IMPLIES THAT WHEN WE ASK God for things, we should ask with good motives, not bad. Here's an example. Let's say I'm single and want to be married. A bad motive would be *so I can be happy* because that makes the relationship all about me and also puts the other person in the God position. I shouldn't need another person to be happy.

A good motive would be *so I can share life with another person*. This motive recognizes that relationships are a give-and-take endeavor. I'll gain things from the relationship, but I'll also have to sacrifice some things.

With this second motive, I'll be in a great position to grow as I'll need to mature so I can love the other person with sacrificial love. With the first motive, I'll be in a great position to live a discontented, resentful life because chances are good that the other person won't make me happy all the time.

8. Let's see what this looks like with your wants. Review what you listed in question 7. What is a good motive for asking God for each of those things? What is a bad motive? (Note: Sometimes it's difficult to come up with a good motive. This could mean a) God doesn't want you to have it, b) God does want this, but He wants you to pursue it with a different motive, or c) God doesn't have an opinion other than He wants you to keep Him first and be kind. For example, in a relationship you often have to take turns getting what you want since you both want different things.)

9. James tells us that when we're friends with the world, we're enemies with God. Often our bad motives reflect the world's priorities, and our good motives reflect God's priorities. Look back at the motives you listed in question 8. How would those good motives enhance your friendship with God?

10. In verse 6, James reminds us that God is opposed to the proud but gives grace to the humble. How would you define the word *proud?* How would you define the word *humble?*

11. What would it look like to pursue the things you listed in question 7 with a prideful attitude? What would it look like to pursue what you want with a humble attitude?

PRAY

12. Read the passage again with your envies in mind, then visit with God about the envies and desires you mentioned in questions 3 and 7. Confess any sinful attitudes and thank God for the blessings He has already given you, then ask Him for wisdom and insight as you think about how to handle those desires.

TAKEAWAY

13. What is your biggest takeaway from today's lesson?

ACTION STEPS

14. List any action steps you'd like to take based on your takeaway and prayer time with God.

FOURTEEN

Spiritual Attack

JAMES 4:7–10

7 Submit therefore to God. Resist the devil and he will flee from you. 8 Draw near to God and He will draw near to you. Cleanse your hands, you sinners; and purify your hearts, you double-minded. 9 Be miserable and mourn and weep; let your laughter be turned into mourning and your joy to gloom. 10 Humble yourselves in the presence of the Lord, and He will exalt you.

 **OBSERVE**

1. Summarize or diagram this passage.

THINK

2. James 4:1–6 talks about envy, lust, and friendship with the world, so when he tells us to resist the devil, it's with that context in mind. Do you think Satan would like us to be filled with envy, lusting for what we don't have, and desiring the things of the world? Why or why not?

3. Think of your life this week. In what ways have you been envying, lusting, and engaging in friendship with the world?

4. How has your envy, lust, and friendship with the world affected your contentment level and relationship with God?

5. James tells us to resist the devil and submit to God. What would submitting to God and resisting the devil look like on a practical level in the situations you mentioned in question 3? (Write down your ideas first, then check out Matthew 4:1–11; Ephesians 6:10–18; and Romans 12:1–2 for more ideas if you need them.)

6. According to James 4:7–8, what will happen if you resist the devil and draw near to God?

7. Sometimes we think the Christian life should be easier, but it takes energy and work to resist the devil. Remember Jesus in the desert? He was so worn out after forty days of resisting Satan that the angels had to come and minister to him (Matthew 4:11). What will you gain if you put effort into both resisting the devil and drawing near to God?

8. Sometimes when we're working on an area of our lives to bring it into submission to God, things seem to get worse before they get better. According to verses 8–10, what kinds of hard things often happen when we resist the devil and draw near to God?

9. According to today's passage, what good things will happen if we persevere? (See also James 1:2–4 and Galatians 5:22–23.)

🍃 PRAY

10. Read the passage again with your temptations in mind, then visit with God about your ideas for resisting the devil (see question 5). Ask Him for wisdom and strength, then thank Him for being a grace-filled God who loves you and delights in you (Psalm 18:19; Hebrews 4:15–16).

 **TAKEAWAY**

11. What is your biggest takeaway from today's lesson?

 **ACTION STEPS**

12. List any action steps you'd like to take based on your takeaway and prayer time with God.

FIFTEEN

Letting Go of Judgment

JAMES 4:11–12

11 Do not speak against one another, brethren. He who speaks against a brother or judges his brother, speaks against the law and judges the law; but if you judge the law, you are not a doer of the law but a judge of it. 12 There is only one Lawgiver and Judge, the One who is able to save and to destroy; but who are you who judge your neighbor?

OBSERVE
1. Summarize or diagram this passage.

🌿 THINK

2. Sometimes it's hard to tell when we're judging people. How do you know when you've crossed the line between recognizing sin and judging the person who is sinning (or has some weakness or personality trait you don't like)?

OFTEN WE KNOW we've slipped into judgment when we catch ourselves thinking, *He's such a jerk!* or *I can't believe she did that!* At that point we're not seeing the other person as a fellow sinner; instead, we're (subconsciously) thinking, *That person is way worse than me.* Another way we can tell we've slipped into judgment is when we find ourselves writing people off and thinking they're stupid, crazy, or ridiculous. Letting go of judgment is a lot of work, yet James tells us not to judge.

3. According to this passage, why aren't we supposed to judge people?

WHEN WE JUDGE OTHERS, it's like the person in prison for tax evasion judging the person in prison for stealing from the convenience store. He would have no place to judge because he's a fellow sinner! God is the only One in a position to judge because He's the only One who hasn't sinned. Let's see what this looks like in our lives.

4. Who have you been judging lately, and what have you been judging them for? Be specific and try to think of several examples.

5. Now think of your own faults and sins. Can you think of any ways you're similar to the people you judge? Things people could judge *you* for? For example, I tend to judge my husband for his slow driving, but he could judge me for my fast driving! Review question 4 and list a few of the ways you're similar to people you judge. (If you can't think of any ways, list some other faults or sins people could judge you for.)

6. What happened when you started thinking of your own sins and faults?

7. James 4:7 says if we judge the law, we're not a doer of the law but a judge of the law. In Matthew 7:1–5, Jesus tells us to take the log out of our eyes before we try to take the speck out of another's eyes. Why do you think Jesus and James want us to focus on our faults rather than the faults of others? List several reasons, if possible.

8. Even though we know we shouldn't dwell on the sins and faults of others, it's easy to get swept up into the habit. In the last week, how many minutes (or hours) have you spent dwelling on the faults of others or chatting with a friend or family member about the faults of others?

9. How many minutes during the last week have you spent working on your sins and faults?

10. How would your life change if you were to spend as much time working on your own sins and faults as you currently do focusing on the sins and faults of others?

🍃 PRAY

11. Read the passage again with the people you tend to judge in mind, then spend time confessing your sins and asking God to help you change. Then pray for the person you're judging, asking God to help him or her change as well. Finally, thank God for the good qualities in the person you're judging.

 **TAKEAWAY**

12. What is your biggest takeaway from today's lesson?

 **ACTION STEPS**

13. List any action steps you'd like to take based on your takeaway and prayer time with God.

SIXTEEN

Pursuing Goals

JAMES 4:13–17

13 Come now, you who say, "Today or tomorrow we will go to such and such a city, and spend a year there and engage in business and make a profit." 14 Yet you do not know what your life will be like tomorrow. You are just a vapor that appears for a little while, and then vanishes away. 15 Instead, you ought to say, "If the Lord wills, we will live and also do this or that." 16 But as it is, you boast in your arrogance; all such boasting is evil. 17 So for one who knows the right thing to do and does not do it, for him it is sin.

 **OBSERVE**

1. Summarize or diagram this passage.

THINK

2. What type of person is James talking to in this passage?

3. Do you think this passage is saying we can't make goals and plans? Explain.

4. Let's see what James's advice looks like with some of our goals. List a few of your current goals. Think of both work-related goals and personal goals.

5. Choose one or two of your goals from the previous question. What would it look like to pursue your goal(s) with this passage in mind?

6. How do you think pursuing your goal(s) that way would affect your a) attitude, b) pursuit of the goal, and c) relationship with God as you work on your goal(s)?

7. James 4:16 mentions arrogance and boasting. How would you define arrogance? How would you define *boasting?*

8. Review your definitions of boasting and arrogance, then think of the goals you mentioned in question 5. In what ways have you been arrogant or boastful with your goals?

OFTEN WE BOAST because we want people to think well of us. When we feel like they're *not* thinking well of us, we go into boasting mode. Subconsciously, we think that if we can just show them what we've accomplished, they won't think so poorly of us. Other times we boast because we feel like we have to be great to be acceptable, and we think boasting will show people we're great. Let's see how this plays out in real life.

9. Do you think boasting usually makes people think well of us? Why or why not?

10. How is boasting to make others think well of us different from the attitude of Jesus in Matthew 20:26–28?

11. Now think of your goals. What would it look like to pursue your goals from a servant's heart? What would it look like to pursue them from a looking-good-in-the-eyes-of-others heart?

 **PRAY**

12. Read the passage again with your goals in mind, then spend time visiting with God about your goals. Ask Him to help you pursue your goals with a servant's heart, leaning on Him to accomplish them, yet holding the outcome with open hands.

TAKEAWAY
13. What is your biggest takeaway from today's lesson?

ACTION STEPS
14. List any action steps you'd like to take based on your takeaway and prayer time with God.

SEVENTEEN

Holding Money with Open Hands

JAMES 5:1-6

1 Come now, you rich, weep and howl for your miseries which are coming upon you. 2 Your riches have rotted and your garments have become moth-eaten. 3 Your gold and your silver have rusted; and their rust will be a witness against you and will consume your flesh like fire. It is in the last days that you have stored up your treasure! 4 Behold, the pay of the laborers who mowed your fields, and which has been withheld by you, cries out against you; and the outcry of those who did the harvesting has reached the ears of the Lord of Sabaoth. 5 You have lived luxuriously on the earth and led a life of wanton pleasure; you have fattened your hearts in a day of slaughter. 6 You have condemned and put to death the righteous man; he does not resist you.

OBSERVE
1. Summarize or diagram this passage.

🍃 THINK

2. Why do you suppose the wealthy people in this passage are storing up riches for themselves and not paying their workers enough?

3. My guess is that you're not using your riches to put righteous people to death or withholding the pay of the people who are mowing your fields, but it can be helpful to consider how we do spend our riches. List all of the reasons you would like to have (or enjoy having) a lot of money.

4. Verse 5 talks about living for pleasure and living luxuriously. Think of your experience with living for pleasure, not just on vacation, but all the time. Do you think living for pleasure makes a person happy? Why or why not?

5. One of Jesus's requirements for the men who wanted to be His disciples was that they had to leave their homes and belongings to travel with Him (Matthew 4:18–22, 9:9; Luke 9:57–62). Why do you think Jesus asked that of His disciples?

6. Believers in the early church had a practice of selling all their belongings and pooling their finances to serve the church as a whole (Acts 2:42–45). Why do you suppose the disciples set up the church that way?

7. Picture yourself traveling with Jesus during His ministry on earth or leaving your current home and living communally with other believers for the purpose of discipleship, ministry, and evangelism. Would you value the same things you valued in question 3? If not, what would you value in this new lifestyle?

I THINK THE MAIN REASON Jesus asked his disciples to give up everything to follow Him is the same reason the early believers lived communally: they wanted to be able to focus on living 100 percent for God—spending time with Him, learning from Him, and sharing His love with others by meeting their physical needs and discipling them (Matthew 6:33; Luke 10:38–42; Matthew 10:5–31). If they'd spent all their time caring for their properties and belongings, they would have been distracted in helping Jesus with His ministry.

8. Now think of your own life and your current ministry or vocation. In what ways do your home, belongings, work, and recreational pursuits *help* you with your ministry/vocation and growing closer to God?

9. In what ways do your home, belongings, work, and recreational pursuits hinder your ministry/vocation or spending time with God? Think about how they cause you to spend your time, make you feel, or the effort you expend to pay for them.

10. If the goal is to be free to focus on loving God and others well (which would include discipleship, spending time with God, learning from God, and ministry), can you think of anything God would want you to spend less money on?

11. If the goal is to love God and others well, can you think of anything God would want you to spend more money on?

 **PRAY**

12. Read the passage again with your spending habits in mind, then visit with God about the things that came up in the last two questions.

 **TAKEAWAY**

13. What is your biggest takeaway from today's lesson?

 **ACTION STEPS**

14. List any action steps you'd like to take based on your takeaway and prayer time with God.

EIGHTEEN

Trials and Maturity

JAMES 5:7–11

7 Therefore be patient, brethren, until the coming of the Lord. The farmer waits for the precious produce of the soil, being patient about it, until it gets the early and late rains. 8 You too be patient; strengthen your hearts, for the coming of the Lord is near. 9 Do not complain, brethren, against one another, so that you yourselves may not be judged; behold, the Judge is standing right at the door. 10 As an example, brethren, of suffering and patience, take the prophets who spoke in the name of the Lord. 11 We count those blessed who endured. You have heard of the endurance of Job and have seen the outcome of the Lord's dealings, that the Lord is full of compassion and is merciful.

 **OBSERVE**

1. Summarize or diagram this passage.

🌿 THINK

2. This passage mentions *patience* four times and *endure* or *endurance* two times. How would you define *patience?* How would you define *endurance?*

3. James gives three examples of people practicing patience and endurance: the farmer, the prophets, and Job. Think of the lives of these people. What trials did they suffer, and what reward did they receive for their suffering? List as many trials and rewards as possible.[7]

	TRIALS	REWARDS
Farmer		
Prophets		
Job		

4. Now think of your own life. List two or three trials you're currently going through. Include trials in your regular life or in your faith, such as doubt, being ridiculed for your faith, or the struggles that come from trying to be faithful (reading your Bible, growing in character, letting go of sin, laying down your life to love others well, etc.).

5. Review your definitions of patience and endurance from question 2. What would it look like on a practical level to be patient and endure each of the trials you just listed?

6. What rewards might you receive if you persevere in your trials? (If you need ideas, review the rewards you listed in question 3 for the farmer, the prophets, and Job.)

7. Endurance and patience offer wonderful rewards, but too often we choose to escape our trials (with food, alcohol, entertainment, etc.) or avoid our trials (leave the situation, don't put any effort into it, etc.) rather than persevering in them. Review questions 3 through 6 and James 1:2–4. What will you miss out on if you try to escape or avoid your trials rather than face them and persevere? What will you have to sacrifice or accept if you persevere?

8. James 5:9 reminds us not to complain against others during trials. Are you mentally or verbally blaming anyone for the trials you mentioned in question 4? If so, who are you complaining against? What would be a more helpful response if you want to receive the rewards you mentioned in the previous question?

9. In today's Bible passage, James tells us to be patient until the coming of the Lord and reminds us that the Lord is full of compassion and mercy. (See also Hebrews 4:15–16.) How would you define compassion? How would you define mercy?

10. What would the Lord's compassion and mercy look like with the trials you mentioned in question 4? Be specific.

 **PRAY**

11. Read the passage again with your current trials in mind, then visit with God about them, thanking Him for His compassion and mercy. Ask Him for help to endure and wisdom in how to proceed.

TAKEAWAY

12. What is your biggest takeaway from today's lesson?

ACTION STEPS

13. List any action steps you'd like to take based on your takeaway and prayer time with God.

Chapter 18 Footnotes

7. If you need help with the prophets and Job, check out these passages for just a sample of their trials and rewards: Job: Job 1:13–2:10; 42:5, 10–17; Prophets: Hebrews 11:23–30; Deuteronomy 34:10; Jeremiah 20; 31:1–20; Lamentations 3:22–25.

NINETEEN

Praying, Praising, and Healing

JAMES 5:12–15

12 But above all, my brethren, do not swear, either by heaven or by earth or with any other oath; but your yes is to be yes, and your no, no, so that you may not fall under judgment. 13 Is anyone among you suffering? Then he must pray. Is anyone cheerful? He is to sing praises. 14 Is anyone among you sick? Then he must call for the elders of the church and they are to pray over him, anointing him with oil in the name of the Lord; 15 and the prayer offered in faith will restore the one who is sick, and the Lord will raise him up, and if he has committed sins, they will be forgiven him.

 **OBSERVE**

1. Summarize or diagram this passage.

THINK

2. In our previous lesson, we talked about persevering during trials. In this lesson, James talks about praying during trials. Let's see what this would look like with our trials. Describe a trial you're going through right now. How are you responding to that trial? (See question 7 in the previous lesson for ideas of how we respond to trials.)

3. What would happen if you were to instead visit with God about your trial, then choose a positive course of action that might help the situation, or work on accepting what you need to accept (we talked about that in Lesson 9) if you're unable to change the situation? (See also Psalm 32:8, 34:17; Isaiah 41:10; Philippians 4:6–7; Hebrews 4:16.

WHEN I VISIT WITH GOD about my trial and try to see it from His perspective, I usually end up far more peaceful. I also end up far more mature because God uses our trials to help us grow when we go to Him for help (James 1:2–4). For example, if it's a relationship trial, God may use that trial to teach us how to give grace, stop people-pleasing, or be less selfish. If it's a trial of feeling overwhelmed with responsibilities, He may want to teach us how to work hard, work less (take some things off our plates), or let go of perfectionism and procrastination. If it's a trial that produces worry, He may want us to learn how to trust Him, take action even when we don't know how things will turn out, or let go and accept that we can't control everything.

4. Think of the trial you mentioned in question 2. Can you think of anything God may want to teach you when you come to Him in prayer for your current trial?

5. How does it change your attitude toward your trial when you think of the ways God could help you grow through it?

6. The next thing James tells us to do is to sing praises when we're cheerful. Record something you're currently happy about. Why do you think it would be helpful to praise God for that?

7. The next topic James brings up is those who are sick. What does James advise, and why do you think that could be helpful?

8. Does James 5:15 mean that anytime we pray in faith, God will heal as long as we have enough faith? Why or why not?

9. Since we know all people eventually die, we know God won't heal every time we ask Him to. What would happen to our attitude and feelings toward God, though, if we did expect Him to heal every time we prayed with faith, and then one day He didn't come through?

10. Is there anyone in your life right now, including you, who needs healing but hasn't been healed? If so, is that affecting your feelings toward God in any way? Explain.

THE THING THAT HELPS ME when I think about my loved ones not being healed is that God uses trials to help believers grow (Romans 5:3–5, 8:28; 2 Corinthians 12:7–10) and unbelievers believe. It also helps me to see how other believers handle trials like that.

11. What did David do when God didn't heal his son (2 Samuel 12:15–23)? Why do you think he was able to do that? (See also Job 1:18–22.)

🌿 PRAY

12. Read the passage again with the current trials, blessings, and health concerns of you or your loved ones in mind. Of all the topics in today's lesson, which one hit you hardest? Visit with God about that topic and ask Him for wisdom and insight in how He wants you to respond.

TAKEAWAY

13. What is your biggest takeaway from today's lesson?

ACTION STEPS

14. List any action steps you'd like to take based on your takeaway and prayer time with God.

TWENTY

Prayers and Confession

JAMES 5:16–20

16 Therefore, confess your sins to one another, and pray for one another so that you may be healed. The effective prayer of a righteous man can accomplish much. 17 Elijah was a man with a nature like ours, and he prayed earnestly that it would not rain, and it did not rain on the earth for three years and six months. 18 Then he prayed again, and the sky poured rain and the earth produced its fruit. 19 My brethren, if any among you strays from the truth and one turns him back, 20 let him know that he who turns a sinner from the error of his way will save his soul from death and will cover a multitude of sins.

 OBSERVE

1. Summarize or diagram this passage.

THINK

2. James begins by telling us to confess our sins to one another and pray for one another. How would you define *confess*? How would you define *pray*?

3. If you've ever confessed your sins to another person, what benefits did you experience from your confession? If you haven't, do you think it could be helpful in any way? Explain.

4. What would keep you from confessing your sins to someone else? Based on your answer, who would you feel safe enough with to confess your sins?

5. Confessing our sins to others can be powerful, but prayer is also powerful. According to your definition of pray in question 2, why do you think prayer is powerful?

6. Read the following Bible verses and list some things God does for us through prayer: Psalm 16:7, Isaiah 41:10, Zephaniah 3:17, John 14:26, Acts 3:19, 2 Corinthians 1:3–4, James 5:16, 1 John 1:9.

7. What do these verses say about who God is and how He wants to interact with us?

8. So often we think of prayer as just asking God for things. What would you miss out on if you only asked Him for things and didn't experience the other aspects of prayer mentioned in the passages in question 6?

9. Even though we can see the benefits of prayer, it can be hard to develop a prayer habit. Or we might be good at praying for ourselves and others but not good at praising God, confessing sins, or just sitting and fellowshipping with God. What types of prayer do you struggle with, and what keeps you from spending time in prayer?

10. If you'd like a little more discipline with prayer, what could you do to remember to pray? List as many ideas as you come up with, then circle the most appealing ones.

11. James 5:19–20 seems an odd tagalong passage as it doesn't seem to immediately tie in with the last few verses. Do you think James is implying that we can help bring wandering souls back to God by praying for them? Also, think of everything you've read in James. If you were to follow all the dos and don'ts of James, would you be better equipped to help wandering souls come back to God? Why or why not?

 PRAY

12. Read the passage again with your own prayer and confession habits in mind, then visit with God about how you might incorporate prayer and confession into your life.

 **TAKEAWAY**

13. What is your biggest takeaway from today's lesson?

 **ACTION STEPS**

14. List any action steps you'd like to take based on your takeaway and prayer time with God.

About the Author

BARB RAVELING is the author of seven books and Bible studies, including *Freedom from Procrastination*, *Freedom from Emotional Eating*, and the *Renewing of the Mind Project*. She is also a Christian life coach and the host of the *Christian Habits Podcast* and *Taste for Truth Podcast* where she helps people break free from their strongholds and grow closer to God.

Other Books by Barb Raveling
Freedom from Procrastination Bible Study and Workbook
Rally: A Personal Growth Bible Study
Renewing of the Mind Project
Taste for Truth Bible Study
I Deserve a Donut (and Other Lies That Make You Eat)
Freedom from Emotional Eating Bible Study

Barb's Podcasts
Christian Habits Podcast
Taste for Truth Podcast

Connect with Barb:
www.barbraveling.com

www.ingramcontent.com/pod-product-compliance
Lightning Source LLC
Chambersburg PA
CBHW031423290426
44110CB00011B/493